Build a House

written and illustrated by
Heinz Kurth

Puffin Books

Puffin Books: Penguin Books Ltd,
Harmondsworth, Middlesex, England
Penguin Books Inc.,
7110 Ambassador Road, Baltimore, Maryland 21207, U.S.A.
Penguin Books Australia Ltd,
Ringwood, Victoria, Australia
Penguin Books Canada Ltd,
41 Steelcase Road West, Markham, Ontario, Canada
Penguin Books (N.Z.) Ltd,
182–190 Wairau Road, Auckland 10, New Zealand

First published by Puffin Books 1975

Copyright © Heinz Kurth, 1975

Printed in Great Britain by
Colour Reproductions Ltd, Billericay, Essex, England

People need houses for shelter and warmth.

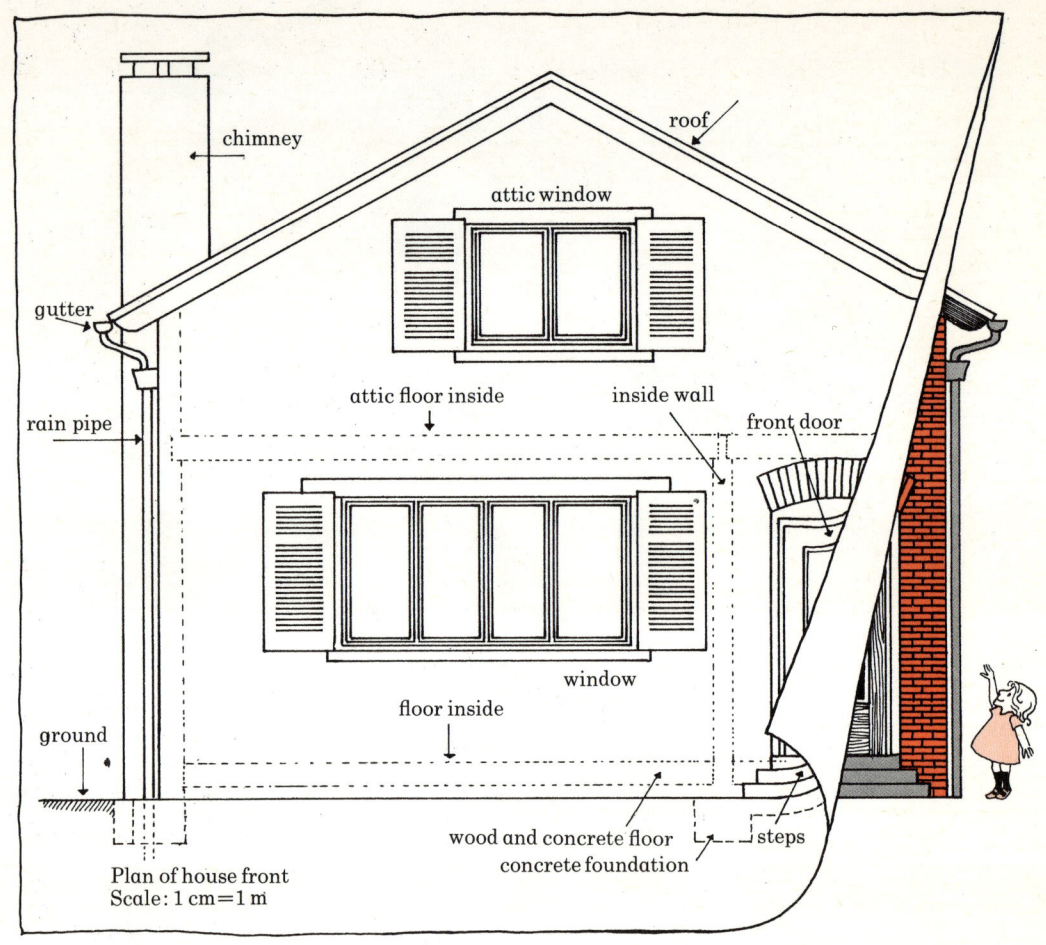

chimney

roof

attic window

gutter

rain pipe

attic floor inside

inside wall

front door

window

floor inside

ground

wood and concrete floor

concrete foundation

steps

Plan of house front
Scale: 1 cm = 1 m

A house starts as a plan drawn by an **architect**.
His plan is drawn to scale. In the plan shown here
the scale is one centimetre to one metre.
This means that the house
will be 100 times larger than this drawing.

A separate plan shows how the walls divide the rooms, and where the doors and windows are to be.

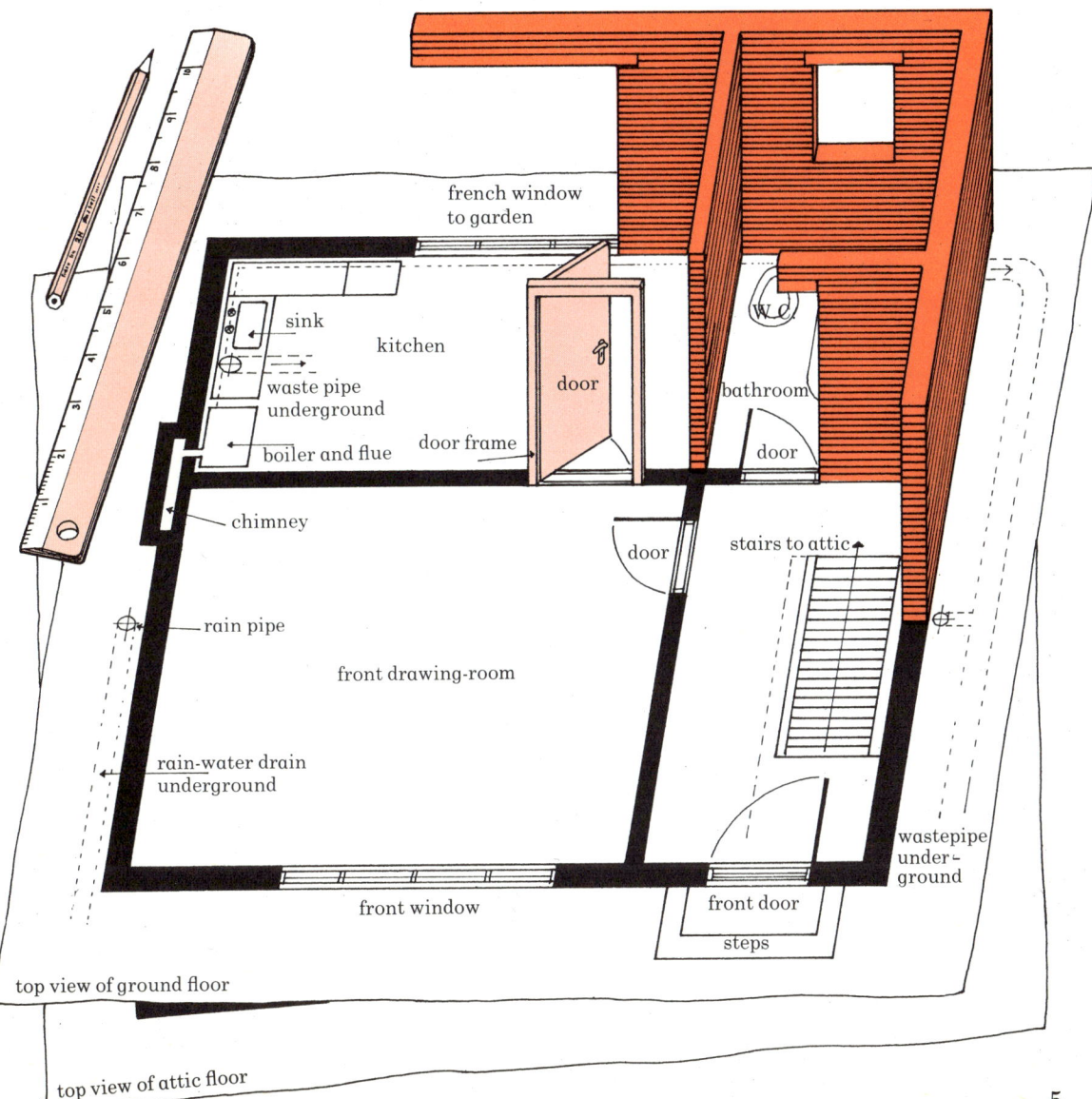

french window to garden

sink

kitchen

waste pipe underground

door

boiler and flue

door frame

W.C.

bathroom

door

chimney

door

stairs to attic

rain pipe

front drawing-room

rain-water drain underground

wastepipe under-ground

front window

front door

steps

top view of ground floor

top view of attic floor

5

This is where the house is to be built.
Workmen are unloading their equipment.

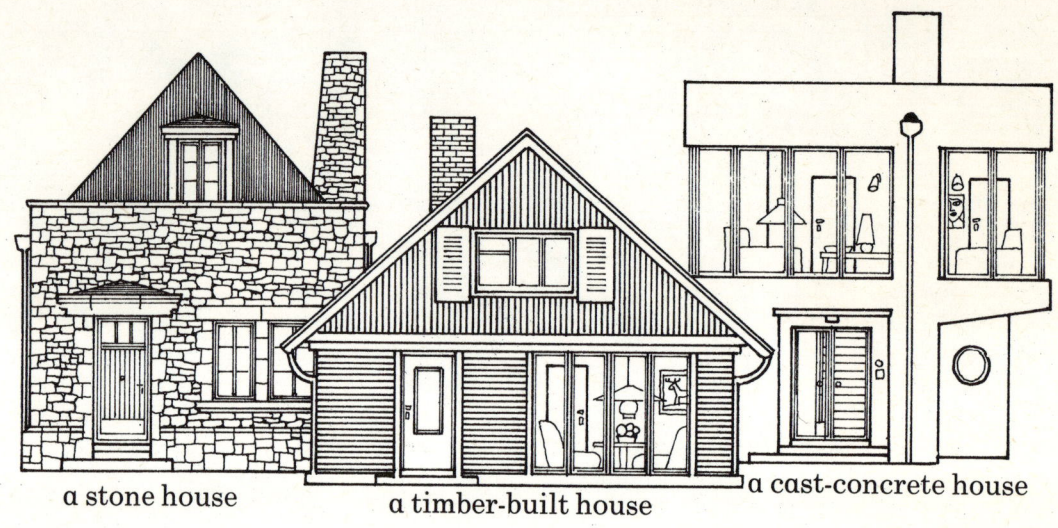

a stone house   a timber-built house   a cast-concrete house

Houses can be built of stone, wood, concrete or brick.
Our house will be built of brick.
Brick walls are built in several ways.

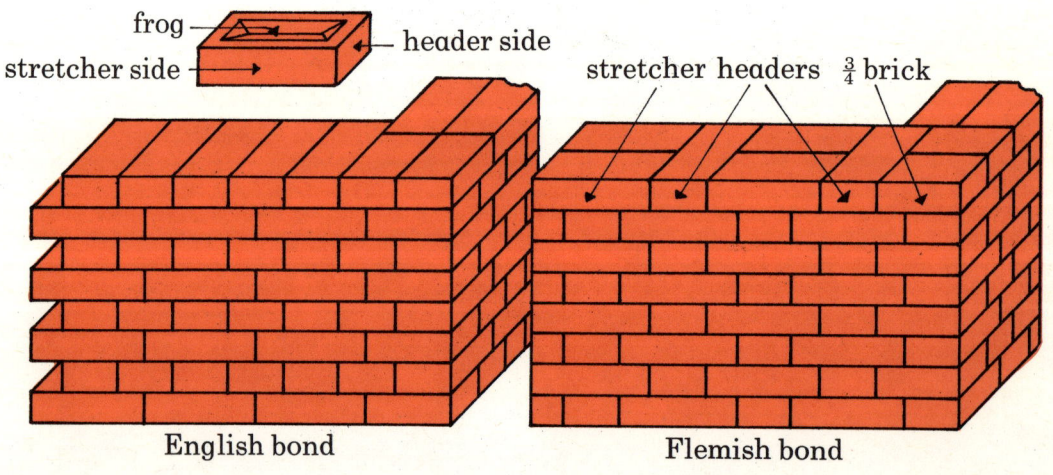

frog —   header side
stretcher side →

stretcher   headers $\frac{3}{4}$ brick

English bond   Flemish bond

Special bricks are made for building different shapes.

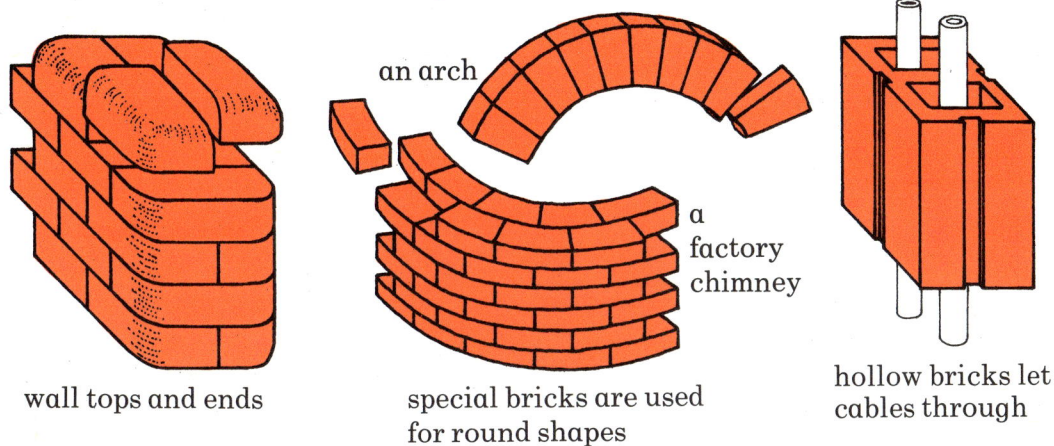

an arch

a factory chimney

wall tops and ends

special bricks are used for round shapes

hollow bricks let cables through

Bricks are held together by **mortar**.
Mortar is a mixture of sand, cement and water.

50 KILOGRAM PORTLAND CEMENT
OPEN HERE

On the building site a large hole is dug in the ground
to make room for the concrete base of the house
on which the bricks will stand.

Trenches are also made for drainpipes, gas and
water pipes, electricity and telephone cables.

A drains
B inspection chamber
C water mains
D gas mains
E electricity mains

Concrete is poured into the hole. It is deeper where
the walls are to be built so that they will not sink or crack.

When the house is finished, all this work will be covered up.

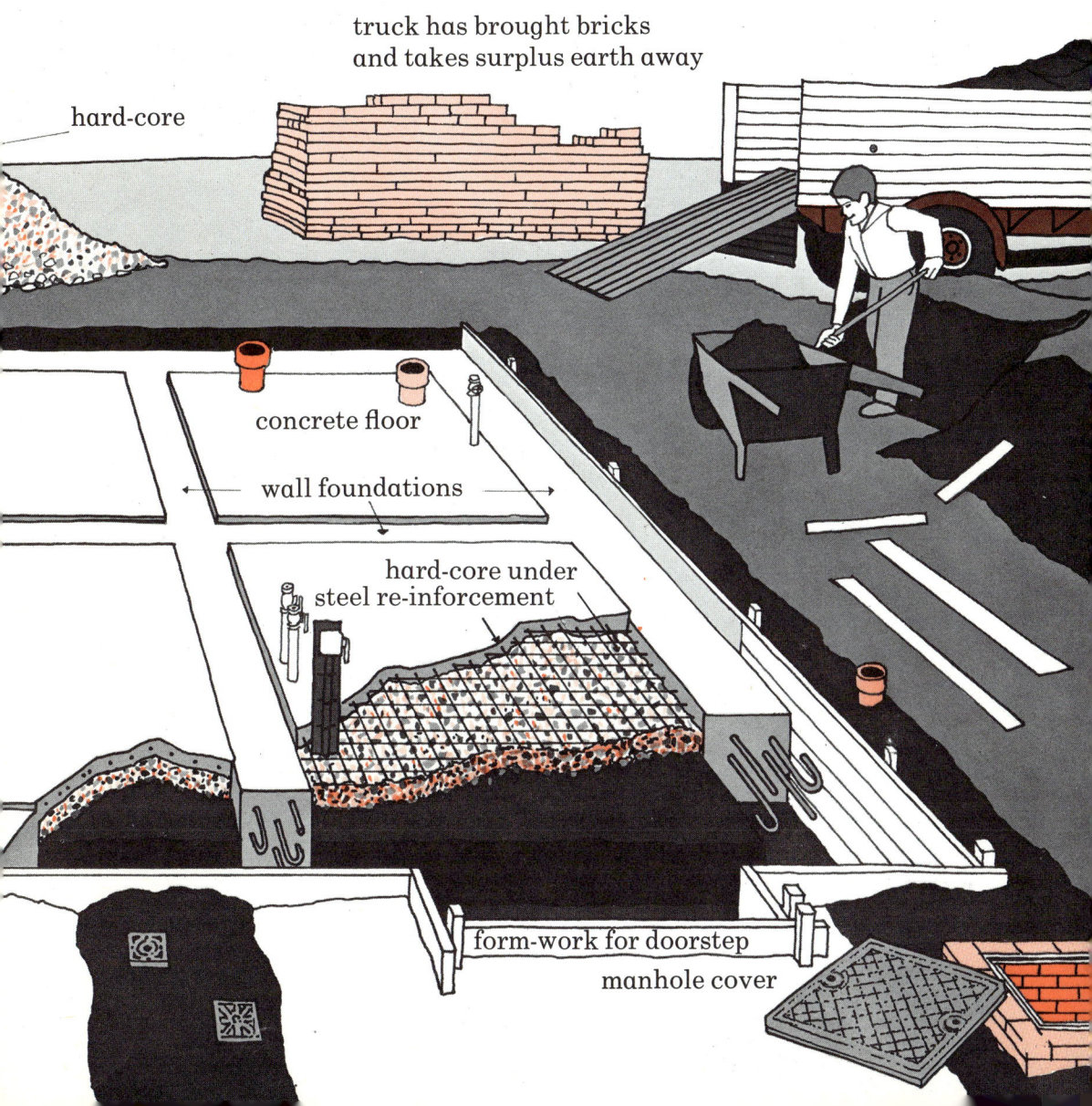

truck has brought bricks and takes surplus earth away

hard-core

concrete floor

wall foundations

hard-core under steel re-inforcement

form-work for doorstep

manhole cover

The **bricklayer** lays the first rows of bricks.
He places a strip of water-proof felt in the wall
to stop the dampness rising up from the earth.

The **builders** follow
the architect's plan
and leave openings in
the walls for the doors
and windows.

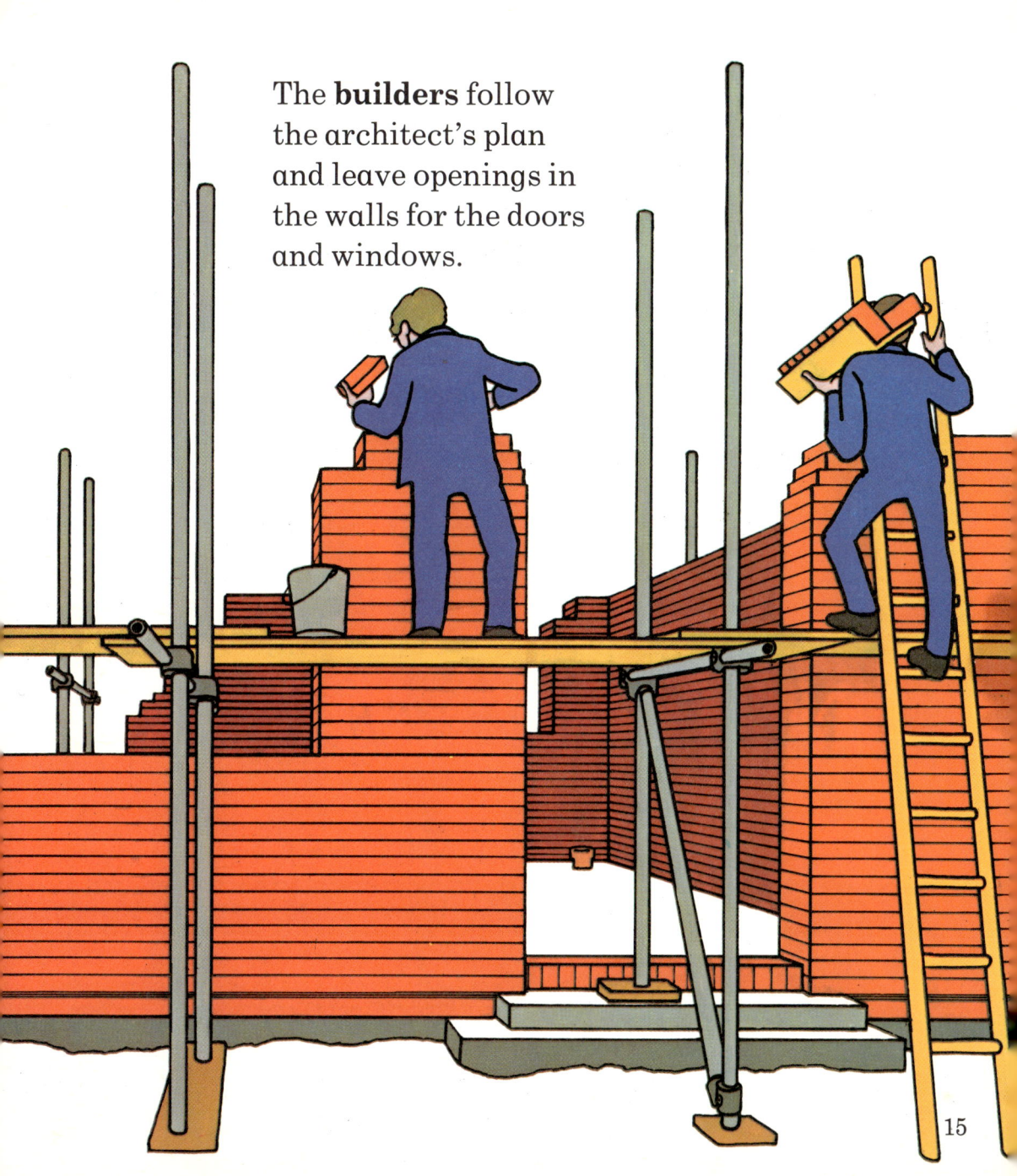

To see that his wall is straight
the bricklayer holds a **plumb-line** against it.
The heavy lead at the end of the string
makes sure it always hangs down in a straight line.

plumb-
line

The outside walls are twice as thick as the inside walls, with a gap in the middle. This gap
stops the cold and rain from getting into the house
and keeps the rooms inside snug and warm.

A beam is placed across
the top of the window
to carry the weight
of the bricks above.
Stone, steel
or concrete beams
are called **lintels**.

Some openings have an arch
above them made of bricks.
They are held in place
by a wooden shape until
the mortar has set.
Then the workmen knock
out the wooden support.

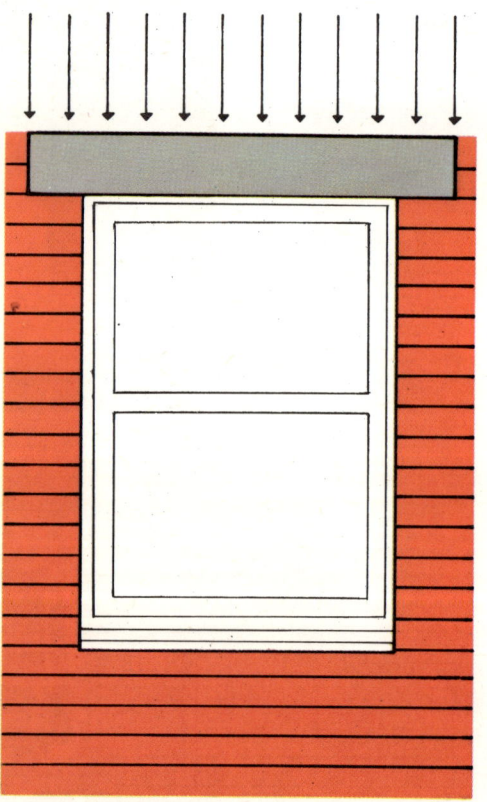

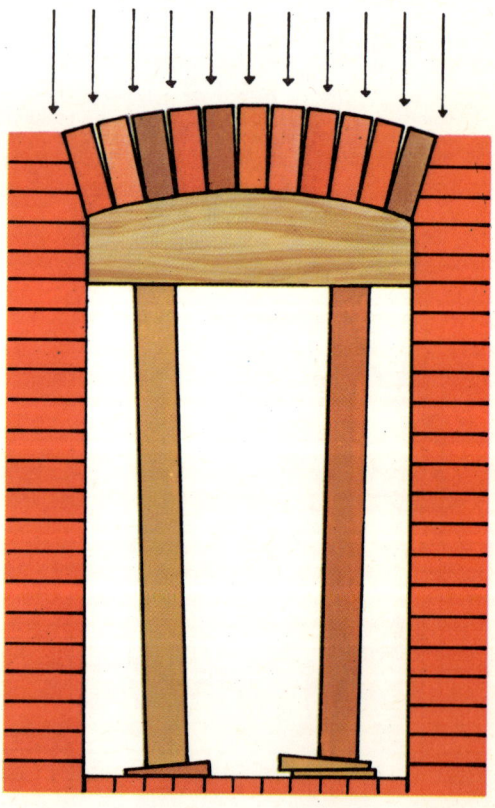

When the **glazier** has put the glass in the windows
he marks it with a white cross
so that the builders will see it and will not knock it out.

Bricklayers are used to working high up. Finishing the chimney is one of the last jobs they do.

flue

boiler

strip-wood flooring
thin tar paint
plastic membrane

concrete floor
skirting board

20

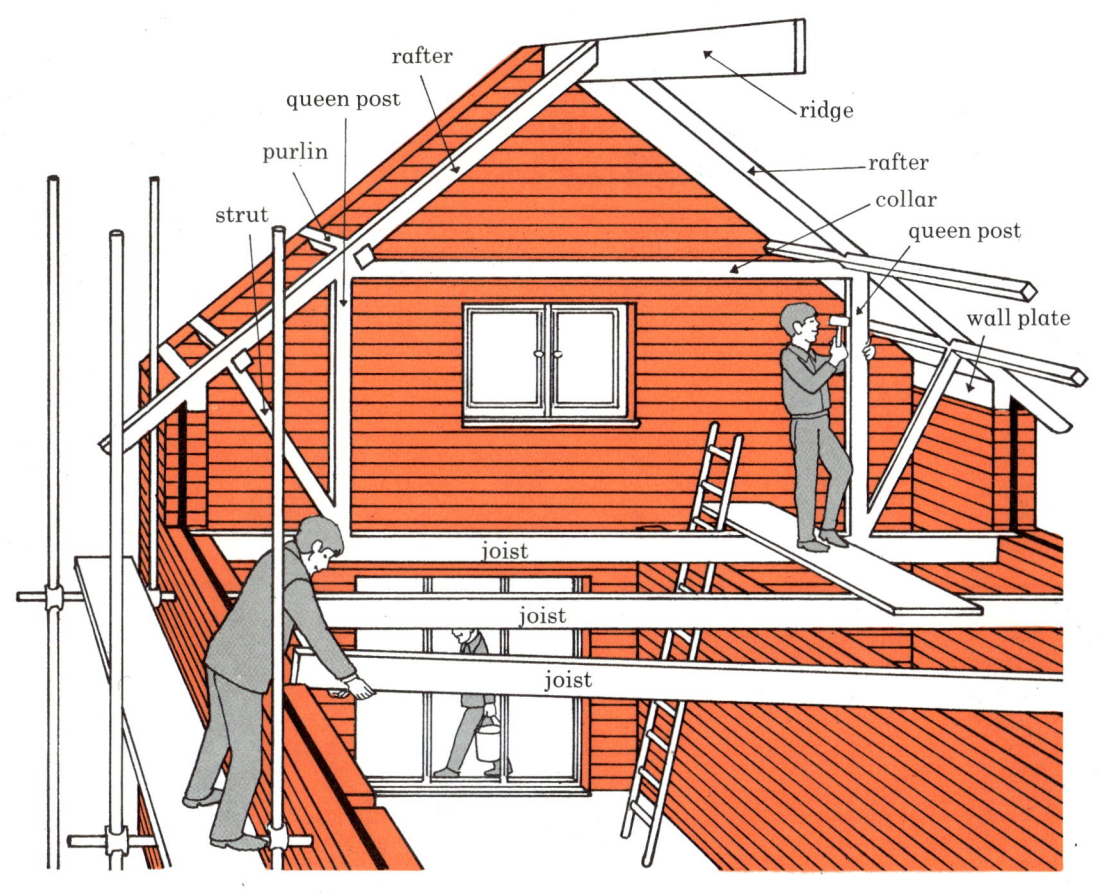

The **carpenter** has put in wood strips on the ground floor.
A row of joists is laid into gaps in the brickwork –
they will hold up the attic floor.
When the rafters for the roof have been put up,
the building begins to look like a house.

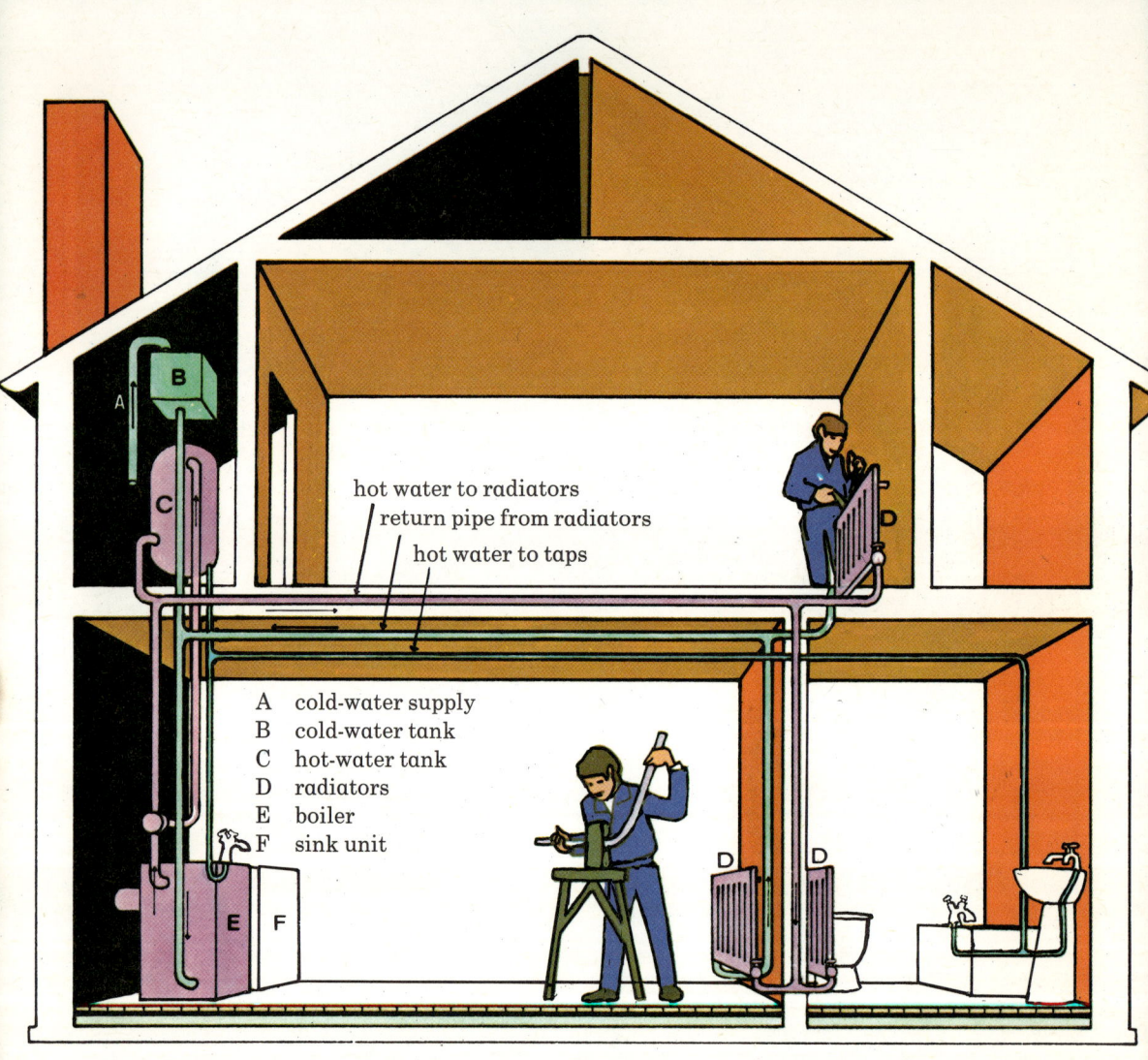

hot water to radiators
return pipe from radiators
hot water to taps

A   cold-water supply
B   cold-water tank
C   hot-water tank
D   radiators
E   boiler
F   sink unit

Now more craftsmen have arrived. The **plumber**
lays the pipes for the bath and sinks.
He also puts in the radiators for the central heating.

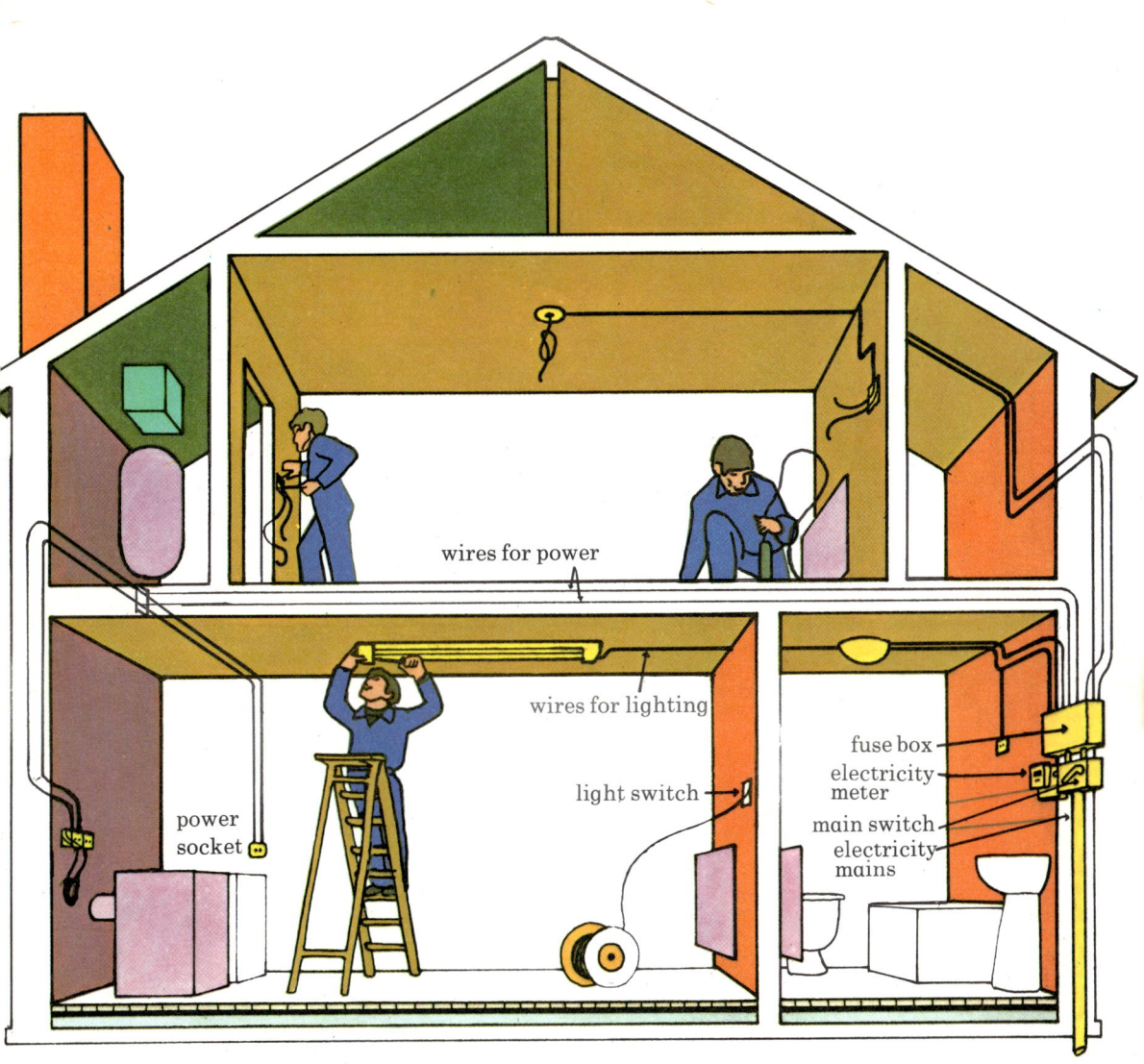

wires for power

wires for lighting

fuse box
electricity meter

light switch

main switch
electricity mains

power socket

The **electrician** fits sockets and switches
and runs wires to all the rooms.

The **plasterer** and his mate have to work fast. They trowel wet plaster on to the walls and smooth it with a float before it sets. This gives a flat finish to the walls.

float

rough mortar on brick wall
soft plaster over mortar
trowel

While the **tiler** is high up on his ladder
hanging roof tiles from wooden slats . . .

A ridge
B rafter
C barge board
D tiling lath
E waterproof sheeting
  or roof felt
F clay tile
G special ridging tile
H gutter
I drain pipe

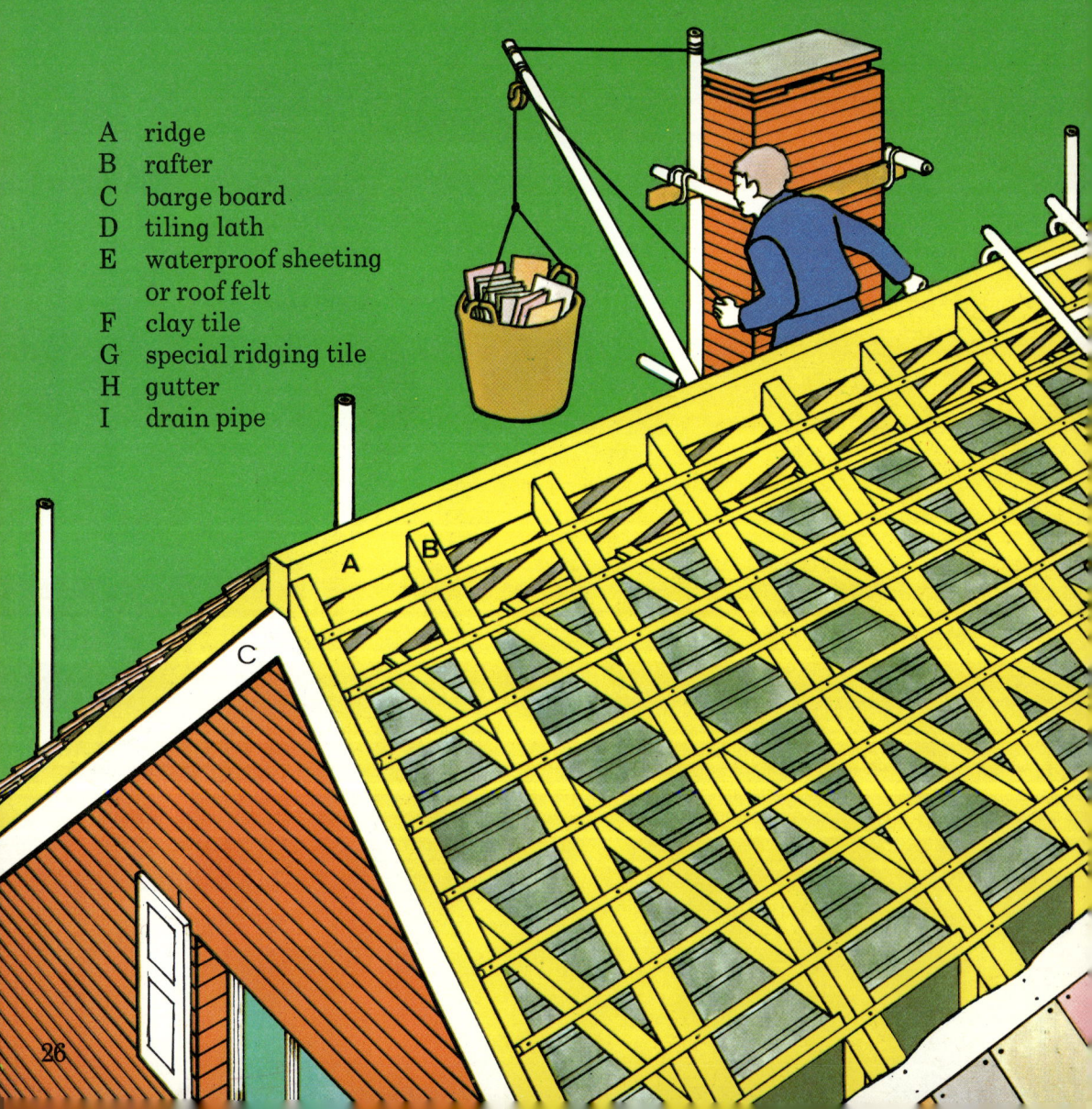

. . . gutters and pipes are bolted on underneath the edge of the roof to carry away the rain water.

Now the plaster is dry
and the **decorators** are hard at work.

They move their trestles from one room to the next,
painting the walls and woodwork.

Finally, the building work
is done and the workmen
are clearing the site.

The house is finished and the new owners
are ready to move in. Their new house
will give them shelter and warmth
for many years to come.